WANT TO GET OUT OF DEBT FAST?

NO PAIN, NO GAIN!

Laura Simmons

Copyright @2019 Laura Simmons

WANT TO GET OUT OF DEBT FAST?

Written by: Laura Simmons
Cover Design by: Sharon Brownlie at

www.aspirebookcovers.com

Printed in the United States of America
ISBN: 9781656583543
All rights reserved solely by the author.
The author guarantees all contents are original and do not infringe upon the legal rights of any other person or work.
No part of this book may be reproduced in any form without the permission of the author. The views expressed in this book are not necessarily those of the publisher.
www.motherdaughterteambooks.com

Mother Daughter Team LLC

DO YOU REALLY WANT TO GET OUT OF DEBT FAST

NO PAIN NO GAIN---

LET ME SHOW YOU HOW I WENT FROM OWING $$$$$$ IN CREDIT CARD DEBT AND HAVING $0.00 IN MY SAVINGS ACCOUNT TO HAVING A NICE SAVINGS ACCOUNT AND INVESTMENTS & BECOMING DEBT FREE ALL IN A MATTER OF 1- ½ YEARS.

Table of Contents

Chapter One 1
Do you really want to get out of debt?? 1
What are you waiting for to get started? 5
Rule Number One: 7
Rule Number Two: 9
KNOW YOUR DEBT SITUATION 11
Financial Fitness Program 15
I Learned To Never Borrow
From Myself Again! 21
Pay Debts When They Are Due 23
When I Decided To Change My Finances 25
Getting On Track Was The
Biggest Step For Me 27
Chapter Two 29
Freezing the cards 29

I had to realize that my money wasn't monopoly money 33
Things I did to get myself out of debt 35
First thing I learned about saving money is: 41
Appendix 1: 52 week Money Plan 59
Appendix 2: Example of a budget......................61
Know your credit Score......................................63

> I've struggled with debt for a long time. Believe me, when I say I wanted to make a change.
>
> —Laura Simmons

I was so tired of going to work every day and I felt like why do I work because at the end of every payday I was broke and when I say broke I mean broke. I would ask my husband for gas money and money to put in my pocket because after battling with credit card debt each month and my other monthly expenses, I would have probably $5.00 or $10.00 to my name. It got to a point that my husband tried to set up a budget for me, but it didn't work. You know why because it has to be something you decide you want to do in order for it to work. You have to be really tired of your situation. It's so easy to for people to say well that's why you have a husband. No, that's not true because what if that marriage doesn't work out or something happens to your spouse, now what are you going to do? Think about that. So we become angry with everyone except ourselves because it seems like you are in a hole that you are never going to get out of, And yeah they say there are programs to help you get out of debt, but guess what they don't tell you they too have a fee that you have to pay them which adds on to your already big black, hole and to top it off, you have to get even deeper in debt before they start helping you get out of debt. Believe me I have tried them and it seemed like my hole got bigger and the harassing calls got even crazier. Every time I got paid I was paying overdraft fees and so on and for and I just got fed up and I sat down one day and put a plan into place and I began to chip at it, but it didn't seem like I was getting anywhere, but that's because I hadn't completely committed to this life change.

You have to commit. You have to figure out the root to how you got here to begin with.

Chapter One

Do you really want to get out of debt??

The first thing you have to do is say that you really want to be debt free and mean it!! If you really want to become debt free, this book will give you ideas for getting out of debt, saving, how to make extra money while you sleep, investing in stocks, getting that credit score up and managing your finances to get a better understanding for yourself. As you begin to clear the debt, you will start noticing the credit score going up. Also keep this in mind it is not going to happen overnight; you didn't rack up the debt overnight so no it is not going to disappear overnight it is a long process and it takes a lot of self-control and commitment.

Also remember,

No Pain No Gain!!

Okay it's time to get to the real nitty-gritty!!

There are things you can do everyday to change your situation.

You are going to learn how to make your money go further for you.

Some things you can do are very small adjustments like changing the thermostat to a lower setting in your home. I changed mine to 70 because I don't like my home to be too hot. You can use your own judgment of what you can set it to you don't have to use mine while we are away we put our thermostat to 50 because no one is there and we don't have any animals. Turn lights out that you aren't using. Cook meals for the entire week and warm them up as you go. Pick one day out the week to do laundry. Make dishwater when do the dishes don't waste dish liquid on individual dishes. Don't let the shower water run for a long time your goal is to wash up and get out of there. See, if you change just a few things in your life it will become an automatic part of your everyday life.

LAURA SIMMONS

What are you waiting for to get started?

You can't manage your finances? You think it's going to be too hard to do?

Or are these four things keeping you from doing it?

1. You have no idea how to plan.
2. No knowledge about how savings and investments work.
3. You leave it up to your significant other or maybe someone else.
4. Or are you just a procrastinator?

Well let me tell you how you can overcome all these things just like I did.

Now remember, No Pain No Gain!!

Everything starts with **you**!!

Make up your mind that this is something you really want to do. It's a great feeling after all the sacrifice you will have to do to watch your bank account go from zero to whatever amount you want it to be.

Then you can sit back and watch your savings account and investments pile up.

Rule Number One:

This will be one of your toughest rules: You can't have everything.

You have to get your priorities in order. The biggest thing for me was asking myself this question: **Do I need this, or do I just want it?**

Rule Number Two:

There are things you may **NEED** like a car to get to and from work. You may want a new BMW, but that's another **want**, not a need.

One of our biggest mistakes is trying to keep up with the Joneses.

The one thing I had to do is break the cycle of thinking I had to have whatever someone else had. Just because my neighbors, friends or even relatives may had them didn't mean I had to have it too. I made up in my mind I wanted to take charge of my financial freedom and raise my credit score.

KNOW YOUR DEBT SITUATION

Here is a quiz you can give yourself to see if your debt situation is really out of control:
Take this quiz-----it will help you to know where you stand with your financial situation.

The answers will go this way:

ALWAYS=3POINTS; OFTEN=2POINTS; SOMETIMES=1POINT; NEVER=0. Get a sheet of paper and a pencil and write down your score after each question. Are You Ready?

1. Your checkbook balance gets lower every month.

2. You can't make it through the month without overdrawing your checking account.

3. You pay the minimum amount due on your credit card bills every month.

4. You are behind on one or more installment payments (i.e., car note or furniture bill.)

5. You are at the limit on your credit cards.

6. You have no (or a very small amount) in your savings account.

7. You count on income from overtime, odd jobs, windfalls or borrowing from family/

friends to get you through the month.

8. You use your credit cards to pay for gas, groceries and even get cash advances to pay for other necessities.

9. You borrow money to pay bills you know are coming up like clockwork every month.

10. You truly don't know how much you owe.

11. You juggle your bills around every month, paying one this month and next month the other one will get paid.

12. You get disconnection and outstanding notices or phone calls.

13. You will sell or pawn your wedding band or family heirlooms to pay your bills.

14. You worry about your bills so much that you argue with your family about money.

15. You think so much about money that you get sick to your stomach thinking about it.

Okay so this is how the scoring system works:

If your total is 15 or below, you're doing great. Now if your total is 16-30, you're average, but you still have some work to do. Now if your total is 30-45, you're walking on really troubled grounds. Now if your total was 45-60 you're in really bad trouble. You need to do something now!!

Financial Fitness Program

This is my 30 days of financial fitness program I did for myself.

I was tired of not having elbow room for myself to even think.

The first thing I did was mentally prepare myself for the in my lifestyle change.

Then I told myself I need a month's vacation from spending.

If you want to you can call it all "diet"-----low funds, instead of low-carbs. Just like with most diets, people will feel sorry for you and at the same time envy your willpower.

The first thing I noticed was that the one-month financial fast gave me time to catch up on bills where I had fallen behind.

Believe me it won't be easy and it won't be pain free! It means cutting out the expensive lunches and bringing that beautiful lunch bag to work everyday with a meal from home, a DVD movie at home, no trips out of town with your friends for a while, no new clothes and bring your bottled water from home. In other words, (NO SPENDING AT ALL!)

Oh yeah, It hurts, but for the most part it was surely a good way to get a fast increase in my cash flow.

You and only you can set a date to begin your money diet. I did the first payday of the month of November 2017. That's when I decided I was going to change my spending habits.

I also set a goal for the money I was going to save. I decided to pay off a big chunk of one of my smallest credit card balances or a bunch of my overdue bills. I even started a real direct deposit savings account where I was putting $25.00 in it every pay period.

Then I made a list of every bill that I had to pay. Not only had I written it down in a book, I decided to get myself a dry marker board and wrote everything that I owed on it so that I could see it whenever I thought about spending money on things I didn't need. This will be a great reminder of how impulsive shopping can put you in debt over your head. I also put a list together that showed everything I really needed to buy, like groceries, gas, deodorant and other personal things. My list that I had written out had every necessity that I needed. When you look at this list again you are going to realize that you have created a budget. This helped me to understand where my money was going. Then I decided to stock up on items and groceries that I needed so that I wouldn't be tempted to impulse shop. I then noticed I had money to pay bills, so I paid as many "must pay" bills as possible on the first day of my spending "vacation."

I paid were all the utilities, cell phones, car payment and any other regular bills. I decided to see what I owed on my cell phones and paid them off so that I would only be charged for usage only. Then, I decided to add extra money to my car note payment each month. I really started understanding my finances so I put all the other expenses such as clothes, movies, restaurants, vacations, and Entertainment miscellaneous things on the back burner. I made up my mind that if it wasn't a necessity, **I DIDN'T NEED TO BUY IT.**

I Learned To Never Borrow From Myself Again!

I had to remind myself that I couldn't borrow from next month's pay either. This helped me to see how much money I had to get through the month, and how much would be left at the end of the month. It wasn't much, but I decided to use the leftover money as part of the 52-week plan. It's a savings club. I realized the "money diet" was truly working for me.

1. I was starting to see I had saved some money.

2. I had mapped out a budget for myself.
3. I was able to see where I was wasting money.
4. I was happy I was changing my spending habits.

I was truly happy to see that I had learned new spending habits that were going to put me back on the right road to financial independence and debt free.

Pay Debts When They Are Due

I don't mean be late with your payments I mean let your money sit in your savings account or checking account for as long as can you so that your money can grow you some interest.

LAURA SIMMONS

When I Decided To Change My Finances-----

I didn't realize I was going to be able to get rid of so many greedy bankers, bill collectors, credit card companies that were in my pockets and the stress that was slowly killing me. It was a mind-blowing experience when I started taking charge of my money.

It made me realize that anyone can get their spending under control and put away money for a rainy day and still live well. Most of the time we think we need to make a lot of money to live well when really we can live well with what we make if we control our spending.

One thing I had to learn is that saving money and spending less doesn't mean living without style and comfort. It's like going to library to check out a movie that you would normal pay for through a red box or purchase it from the store.

Just because you checked it out the library instead of the other places doesn't mean you changed your lifestyle it just means you saved yourself some money by doing so.

Getting On Track Was The Biggest Step For Me

It felt so good when I realized that I had jump-started financial plan with a money diet. I even noticed the major improvement with my credit rating and paid a few bills. It made me want to go on with my plan to make myself financially secure. It was the must empowering moment in my life. You don't realize how much stress is released when debt is gone.

LAURA SIMMONS

Chapter Two

Freezing the cards

I remember how I felt before I started my money diet. I was sinking in quicksand under a load of credit card debt when I decided it was time to get out from underneath it. I stopped buying groceries, gas and restaurant food with my credit cards.

I fell deep into depression when my mom passed and that's when the impulsive shopping began. Some call it therapy shopping.

The reason I mention that is because you really need to know the root of your spending mine was the loss of a loved one.

So I had to realize that I was the only person that could get myself back on track.
Once I paid off some of my credit card balances, I decided to shred the cards. However, I didn't get rid of all my credit cards because we live in a world where credits cards are needed for some things.

So, I decided to keep one active card and I froze it. (literally) I would keep it in a frozen cup of water and in order to use it I had to defrost it, which took time to do.

This way by the time it thawed out, I could have changed my mind about using it which is good because most of the time we tend to spend more when we are using a credit card than we would if we were using cash.

I had to realize that my money wasn't monopoly money

That's when it really got real to me. See I forgot just like most of us forget that plastic will have to be paid for with real dollars, We tend to spend more with a credit card then we would with our cash.

That's when I realized that when I use a credit card I was really just borrowing money------taking out a loan, which had a really high interest, and I was responsible for paying it back. I found myself owning a wallet full of credit cards, which had outstanding balances on every one of them.

Yes, I said every one of them!
I am not going to lie to you; it was madness seeing myself sinking more and more into debt. The funny thing is there are real reasons why you need a credit card and that is for use as Identification in some situations, i.e. for hotels and to rent a car, but now you can actually use a prepaid card for some of these things. This means you can only use what you put on the prepaid credit card. Love it!!

Things I did to get myself out of debt

1. I started calling the credit card companies and asking for a lower interest rate.
2. When I would get the invites to transfer balance to a zero percent interest rate for a year I would take it and focus on paying the debt off before the zero percent interest rate change.
3. I took on an extra job.
4. I started hustling even more by selling items on online Ebay, Posh and other online stores to help me bring in extra income.
5. Then, I cut my spending out all together. I

took the extra money that I was making from the online sales and started adding it to my savings and putting it towards my smallest bills first. After that, it was time to hit the bigger bills and so on. Every step of the way I had a plan in place because I was determined to get out of debt. I got sick and tired of working, but not having anything to show for it and robbing Peter to pay Paul, and the sad part was I hid my credit card debt from everyone I loved because I didn't know how to tell anyone what I had done. Honestly, I was embarrassed and I didn't know how I had gotten there or how I was going to get out of it. I prayed about it (but prayer without work is dead.) I cried about it, but that didn't wash the debt away. So that's when I decided I had enough!

It was truly a process, but I was truly determined to be debt free.

I even learned how to say no to people when they asked to borrow or invited me out to dinner. I was so conscious even about where I withdrew money from as well because those $2.00, $3.00 and $5.00 fees add up quickly. So I learned to carry enough cash with me when I went places because I didn't like paying these greedy banks a fee for using their ATMs.

See, when you know better you tend to do better so as I was going through my debt free journey I found myself watching every penny that I spent. I learned to pick up the phone and call the bank about waiving fees that I may see on my bank statement and to my surprise they would waive the fees that had been applied to my accounts.

It got really real when I got fed up with being broke and all this extra "weight" strapped to me from my debt. So I started noticing everything. I even called the light company or the gas company and questioned my bills. Guess what? They made a mistake on some of my charges and had to send me another bill that was a lot lower than the original bill I had received. I say this to you so that you can start making changes to how you read your bills.

Pay attention to your bills, extra fees, rates and taxes. Sometimes mistakes are made. You have the right to question where your hard earned money is going.

I remember thinking to myself why does it seem like the month is longer than my money each month I felt like this until I started learning how to put my money on a diet.

That's when I was determined to learn how to save some money, which I was never really good at doing. This is really surprising because my mom was really great at saving money.

Save! I use to watch Suzie Orman every Saturday night and I would hear her talk about how you should have 6 months of your wages in a savings account for emergencies.

I said now how am I going to be able to save money when I'm barely keeping my head above water now. When in fact there was money left on the table after paying my bills, but I couldn't see it because I didn't have a budget in place to do so. Now, I can take my smallest income and save a surprising amount of money all because I learned to manage the money I already had.

First thing I learned about saving money is:

I remember hearing most financial advisors saying the first thing you should do when you get paid is pay yourself. Why? Because I worked hard for my income. So, I knew I had to start saving money now, I realized that there was a choice to be made. One thing I had to ask myself was this essential expense?

I had to ask myself if this was something I wanted or something I needed? I learned why my salary wasn't stretching from pay period to pay period. It didn't mean insufficient funds; it honestly meant the timing of my expenses with the arrival of my paycheck was off.

It also let me know that I was spending more than what I had. One thing I realized that I needed to do is pay myself first when I got paid. I owed that to myself. So I did. I set up an amount every payday thereafter. I went so far as to setup my direct deposit to make sure that money was going into my savings account every pay period.

This helped with the need for willpower.

I started seeing my savings account as a bill. As a matter of fact, it is my number one bill in my mind. I learned to start off saving small and eventually I moved my amount up to a larger amount once all my debts were paid in full.

I even saved my change and would cash it in at the end of the week or sometimes at the end of the month. See I don't have any shame to pick up a penny off the ground. Those pennies add up and they eventually turn into dollars. Stop thinking you're too good to pick up a penny off the ground.

You would be surprised how much change you will have at the end of the week just from finding change on the ground alone.

Here's a funny memory, I remember one morning I stopped at the gas station and I saw a penny on the ground. Well, to make a long story short, there were a whole lot of pennies on the ground and people just walked past them, but I stopped and picked up every last one of those pennies and I didn't have any shame in my game.

When it was all said and done, I had collected $3.75 worth of pennies. I have a habit of picking up change off the ground and putting it in a coin holder inside my car. I added that change with what I found in the parking lot of the gas station and I couldn't believe I had $10.00. I took that $10.00 dollars worth of change, cashed it in and saved it until I had $25.00. Then, I deposited that into my savings account. This is something I do every week now. So once a month, I cash my change in at the bank and it goes right into my savings account. Now if I haven't convinced you yet how important it is to save, start figuring out how much you stand to lose by putting it off even one more year.

No, I'm not on the Forbes magazine yet. All that means is that I just have to keep making more income, extra money and continue hustling. I have gotten out of debt, but you best believe I am more conscious about how I spend my money. I utilize every hour of the day. I have learned how to earn extra money at home without quitting my regular jobs. The key is finding just a few hours a week. There are lots of side hustles you can do from home like setup a photo shoot for the local children and women in your community for a small fee, write stories for a local magazine company, make cakes or pies and sell them to your co-workers, family or friends, start a cleaning service or helping your local seniors with their shopping. There are so many ways to make extra money.

This is the best part though. Once you have paid off all your debt, you may want to continue doing these odd jobs to continue building your savings accounts and your investment accounts. You may want to set a goal, to purchase your first home, a new car, or save for that dream vacation.

You can also do what I am doing, saving for that early retirement. With all the things I mentioned in this book, you're on your way to living a better life if that's what you want!

```
Okay guys here's a summary of
what I did:
```

Monthly Budget

Rent or mortgage

Light Bill

Gas Bill

Cell Phone Bill

Fuel for car

Auto Insurance

Groceries

Water Bill

Miscellaneous expenses

Deodorant, toothpaste, body wash etc…

Total monthly bills: ……….

This total is how much you need to save up for 6 months in order to have a 6 months' emergency fund account.

Credit Card Debt

Tackle the smallest credit card balance first Then tackle the next one and so on until you have cleared every credit card balance that you have. Now can't you breathe? And you can really smell the flowers and guess what…. your stress level has gone down. Seriously, credit card debt can really stress you out.

Savings Account

I started out with the 52-week plan. I loved it because you can start with $1, then as you start seeing more of your money you can add on extra.

Here is an example of the 52-week money plan:

Week 1: $1.00 balance: $1.00

Week 2: $2.00 balance $ 3.00

Week 3: $3.00 balance $ 6.00

Week 4: $4.00 balance $ 10.00

Week 5: $5.00 balance $ 15.00

You get the point. Check the appendixes for examples.

Investing

There are several investing companies you can go through to start investing into your future like Robin Hood, Coin Base, Stash, Acorn, 401k, Profit Sharing & more but don't just take my word for it, do your research before investing into anything. Just because it worked for me doesn't mean it will work for you. Learn and study before investing into anything.

Side Hustles

Find things you are good at and make it work for you!

Sell things you don't use or wear anymore on Posh, Ebay, Facebook, Instagram and more. Again, do yourself a favor and make sure you do your research!!

Good luck on your new Debt Free journey!

WANT TO GET OUT OF DEBT FAST?

Follow us on instagram:

Http://instagram.com/Motherdaughterteambooks

Facebook:

Http://facebook.com/themother-daughterteam

Website:

www.motherdaughterteambooks.com

Appendix 1
52 week Money Plan

52 Week Money Challenge Saving Plan

week	Amount Deposited	Account Balance	Week	Amount Deposited	Account Balance
1	$1.00	$1.00	27	$27.00	$378.00
2	$2.00	$3.00	28	$28.00	$406.00
3	$3.00	$6.00	29	$29.00	$435.00
4	$4.00	$10.00	30	$30.00	$465.00
5	$5.00	$15.00	31	$31.00	$496.00
6	$6.00	$21.00	32	$32.00	$528.00
7	$7.00	$28.00	33	$33.00	$561.00
8	$8.00	$36.00	34	$34.00	$595.00
9	$9.00	$45.00	35	$35.00	$630.00
10	$10.00	$55.00	36	$36.00	$666.00
11	$11.00	$66.00	37	$37.00	$703.00
12	$12.00	$78.00	38	$38.00	$741.00
13	$13.00	$91.00	39	$39.00	$780.00
14	$14.00	$105.00	40	$40.00	$820.00
15	$15.00	$120.00	41	$41.00	$861.00
16	$16.00	$136.00	42	$42.00	$903.00
17	$17.00	$153.00	43	$43.00	$946.00
18	$18.00	$171.00	44	$44.00	$990.00
19	$19.00	$190.00	45	$45.00	$1,035.00
20	$20.00	$210.00	46	$46.00	$1,081.00
21	$21.00	$231.00	47	$47.00	$1,128.00
22	$22.00	$253.00	48	$48.00	$1,176.00
23	$23.00	$276.00	49	$49.00	$1,225.00
24	$24.00	$300.00	50	$50.00	$1,275.00
25	$25.00	$325.00	51	$51.00	$1,326.00
26	$26.00	$351.00	52	$52.00	$1,378.00

52-Week Savings Challenge

Week	Date	Deposit	Bal	✓	Week	Date	Deposit	Bal	✓
1					27				
2					28				
3					29				
4					30				
5					31				
6					32				
7					33				
8					34				
9					35				
10					36				
11					37				
12					38				
13					39				
14					40				
15					41				
16					42				
17					43				
18					44				
19					45				
20					46				
21					47				
22					48				
23					49				
24					50				
25					51				
26					52				

Appendix 2
Example of a budget

PROJECTED MONTHLY INCOME				PROJECTED BALANCE			
	Income 1			ACTUAL BALANCE			
	Extra income			DIFFERENCE			
	Total monthly income						
PROJECTED MONTHLY INCOME							
	Income 1						
	Extra income						
	Total monthly income						

HOUSING	Projected	Actual	Difference	ENTERTAINMENT	Projected	Actual	Difference
Mortgage or rent				Video/DVD			
Phone				CDs			
Electricity				Movies			
Gas				Concerts			
Water and sewer				Sporting events			
Cable				Live theater			
Waste removal				Other			
Maintenance or repairs				Subtotals			
Supplies				LOANS			
Other				Personal			
Subtotals				Student			
TRANSPORTATION				Credit card			
Vehicle payment				Credit card			
Bus/taxi fare				Credit card			
Insurance				Other			
Licensing				Subtotals			
Fuel				TAXES			
Maintenance				Federal			
Other				State			
Subtotals				Local			
PETS				Other			

Know your credit Score

Know your credit score by going to these three major credit bureaus.

3 major Credit Bureaus

TransUnion

Experian

Equifax

WANT TO GET OUT OF DEBT FAST?

www.ingramcontent.com/pod-product-compliance
Lightning Source LLC
Chambersburg PA
CBHW070454220526
45466CB00004B/1820